I could write a lengthy novel on reasons to fall in love with Paris. One of the city's greatest traits is the way it opens up and allows you to discover what's to love about it on your own. Surprisingly smaller than you might expect, it's easy to navigate on foot, and very efficient in terms of public transport. Each of the 20 arrondissements spiraling out like an escargot from the center blend seamlessly into one another but with their own distinct character. For Parisians and travelers alike, the neighborhoods you choose are telling of your style and interests. The traditional west is upscale and caters to fine tastes, while the emerging east can be gritty but budding with some of the city's leading culture.

Parisians are not as rude as has been said, and most days the city fully justifies being regarded as one of the most beautiful in the world. It's known as a place for lovers, but I beg to differ. Paris is for bon vivants traveling in good company or on their own. Those who wander with their eyes wide open, enjoy every last bite, drink every last drop, and love with all their hearts. This guide includes some of the places I have discovered doing just that.

———— • ————

the hunt paris writer

haleigh walsworth

Haleigh Walsworth is a writer and photographer who moved to Paris on a whim. A bit of a romantic
to live. Now a true Franco
capital after just six year
her blog, makingmagique
she found her way throug
producing lifestyle conte
When not at work in Paris
Marais drinking lo.

D1359891

where to lay your weary head

Rest up, relax and recharge

HÔTEL THOUMIEUX

CARON DE BEAUMARCHAIS

Step back in time in the Marais

12 Rue Vieille du Temple (75004) / +33 1 42 72 34 12 / carondebeaumarchais.com

Double from €180

Caron de Beaumarchais is a beautiful little hotel in the Marais, with immense charm and character. The *Marriage de Figaro*, Beaumarchais's most famous play, inspired the entire décor: elaborate wallpapers, floral drapes, precious antique furniture and a chandelier decorate each room, most of which have a view of the endearing Rue Vieille du Temple past their prettily planted window box. The owner of the hotel takes great pride in looking after every detail of the interiors as well as for his guests. Perfect for romantics looking for an ode to Paris's past.

HÔTEL AMOUR

Romance in the red light district

8 Rue Navarin (75009) / + 33 1 48 78 31 80 / hotelamourparis.fr

Double from €170

Hôtel Amour fits right in with the ultra stylish neighborhood you'll find it in. While chic and classically Parisian, it's also edgy, taking as it does design inspiration from the gritty sex shops and cabarets that Pigalle has been known for. (Moulin Rouge anyone?) Downstairs, the café and terrace are popular with locals. Upstairs, some of the 24 guest rooms have been decorated by artists, others have been kitted out with curios and erotic photographs. Fun and sensual, it is the ideal bolt-hole for lovers who come to Paris.

HÔTEL CRAYON ROUGE

A playful guesthouse

42 Rue Croix des Petits Champs (75001) / +33 1 42 36 54 19 / hotelcrayonrouge.com

Double from €185

This colorful hotel is located right in the heart of Paris. The walls of the reception and of each of its 17 rooms are covered in creative sketches, giving an artistic touch. The furniture is a mix of modern and retro, with ultra comfortable beds and, to the delight of many foreign tourists, a very modern bathroom. Cheerful and creative, this so called "guesthouse" is inviting for those traveling with children and the young at heart.

HÔTEL DU TEMPS

A bijou retreat

11 Rue de Montholon (75009) / +33 1 47 70 37 16 / hotel-du-temps.fr

Double from €160

Hôtel du Temps is a cozy, newly renovated boutique establishment in Paris's 9th arrondissement. In a city where square-footage is precious, every inch of it here is well appointed. Its 23 sparsely furnished rooms with white walls and white wood floors feel bright and inviting, and are thoughtfully completed with a few worn antiques, wooden desk chairs and exciting textiles. The vintage vibes are stylish, yet the place feels incredibly fresh. The bar downstairs is a nice little hangout as well, and the hotel serves breakfast each morning with fresh pastries from top chef Christophe Michalak.

CARON DE BEAUMARCHAIS

HÔTEL FABRIC

Industrial elegance

31 Rue de la folie Mericourt (75011) / +852 36 78 99 42
splendia.com /en/hotel-fabric-paris

Double from €215

This 33-room hotel near Oberkampf was once a steel factory. Now trendily renovated, the brick walls and abundant space mix original industrial elements with elegant lighting, while bright textiles in the rooms add a pop of color and spice things up a bit. The rooms are comfortable and contemporary, and while there is no restaurant, the neighborhood is home to some of Paris's greatest eats, so good food is never far. The spa and gym are both enticing as well.

HÔTEL THOUMIEUX

Quirky luxury near the Eiffel Tower

79 Rue Saint-Dominique (75007) / +33 1 47 05 49 75 / thoumieux.fr

Double from €245

A lot of people dream of staying at the boutique Hôtel Thoumieux. Not just for its excellent location, but also for its fabulous décor. India Mahdavi's interior design is consummately mismatched with botanical prints and faux animal skins in each room. Rounding off the luxurious feel, the marble bathrooms are stocked with Aesop soaps and lotions. If you feel like staying in, room service is an excellent option, but it would be a shame to miss an opportunity to dine in the Michelin-starred brasserie downstairs during your stay.

RÉSIDENCE NELL

At home in the heart of town

60 Rue Richer (75009) / +33 1 53 24 98 98 / residencenell.com

Double/studio from €300

If you're coming to Paris for an extended stay, Résidence Nell might be the very place to settle in. Their 17 apartments and studios, ideally located in the 9th arrondissement, can host you from one night to one month and even longer if you need. All their interiors are classic, calm and most importantly, comfortable, so you'll be sure to feel right at home. Not without all the advantages of a regular hotel, their services are also customizable. Should you need something during your stay, you can be sure you'll be well looked after.

louvre and montorgueil

In the heart of the Right Bank stands the Louvre museum, yet despite its reputation as one of the world's largest attractions, I dare say it might not be the best the area has to offer. Just behind is the magnificent and less frequented Palais Royal. The quiet inner courtyard of the palace is filled with specialty shops and cafés. In the center is the park, lined with trees that change color in the fall and bloom with magnolias in the spring. It's a lovely place to enjoy some sun when the weather permits. The surrounding neighborhood exudes the same regal quality. Several streets up you'll come across the picturesque Place de Victoires, some of the most coveted properties in the city. Further west is the lively Étienne Marcel area with the bustling Rue Montorgueil boasting an impressive selection of butchers, florists, produce stands and cheese shops. The tiny streets beside it are peppered with trendy independent shops, eateries and bars. If you're in this area, take some time away from the famous art and wander around the whole district to discover its true masterpieces.

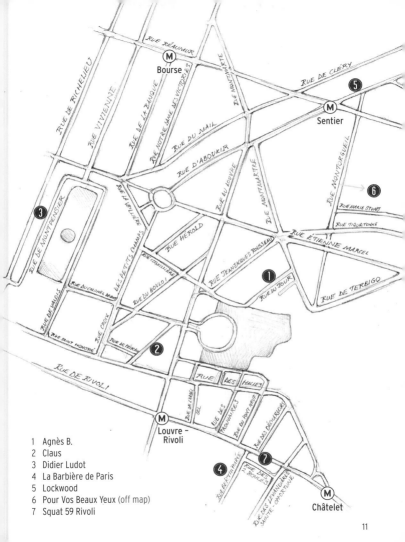

1 Agnès B.
2 Claus
3 Didier Ludot
4 La Barbière de Paris
5 Lockwood
6 Pour Vos Beaux Yeux (off map)
7 Squat 59 Rivoli

11

AGNÈS B.

Culture and cool clothing

6 Rue du Jour (75001) / +33 1 45 08 56 56 / agnesb.fr/boutiques
Closed Sunday

After all these years, Agnès B. is the still the reigning queen of French cutie cool. Nowhere is this more evident than in her flagship store behind Les Halles. She opened her first store right here in 1975, and today the space has grown into a mecca for effortlessly chic male and female Parisians who flock here for clothing and accessories. A cultural sponge and supporter of the arts, the designer's inspirations are reflected in her seasonal collections and also come to life in the store's loft, where you'll find rotating exhibitions she's curated. At the start of each new season, this store is top of my shopping list.

CLAUS
Breakfast in Paris

14 Rue Jean-Jacques Rousseau (75001) / +33 1 42 33 55 10
clausparis.com / Open daily

The French are renowned for their culinary wizardry but breakfast is not their forte. I'm never disappointed with Claus, though, one of Paris's new wave little cafés specializing in all things petit déjeuner. The bright space has the appropriate rise and shine feel to kick-start any day. Downstairs, you can shop from a range of freshly baked goods, muesli and other organic groceries. Upstairs in the salon, you can order your eggs however you like: poached and topped with ham, or perhaps scrambled with bacon on the side? Of course there are plenty of buttery croissants to go around as well, the one breakfast item over which the French are triumphant.

DIDIER LUDOT

House of haute couture

Jardin du Palais Royal, 24 Galerie de Montpensier (75001)
+33 1 42 96 06 56 / didierludot.fr / Closed Sunday

Any vintage collector or admirer must pay a visit to Didier Ludot. Specializing in high-end labels, this is the place to find vintage French couture and high-end ready-to-wear from Chanel, Christian Lacroix, Balmain, Lanvin and more. One of my favorite selections here is the racks of little black dresses, an essential wardrobe piece for every woman. And every woman is guaranteed to find something top-of-the-line and one-of-a-kind in Ludot's fabulous treasury. Once you've fitted yourself out in some chic Parisian attire, the Palais Royal is just the right place to debut your new look.

LA BARBIÈRE DE PARIS

The art of shaving

7 Rue Bertin Poiré (75001) / +33 1 40 26 01 01
labarbieredeparis.com / Closed Sunday and Monday

They say behind every great man is a great woman. In Paris, if you see a man with a ridiculously well kept beard, impeccably trimmed mustache or super clean shave, it's probably true. That's because Sarah has been whipping into shape the facial hair of male Parisians for the last several years at her barbershop. Her handsome and masculine salon is the go-to spot for a shave or trim for him. She and her other barbers will help you choose the best facial hair style for you and work with you over time to achieve it. They're always up to speed on new trends. Once you've grown the desired look, you can make sure it's well maintained with their grooming products.

LOCKWOOD

Dining and drinking around the clock

73 Rue d'Aboukir (75002) / +33 1 77 32 97 21
lockwoodparis.com/bar / Closed Sunday

It's a good thing Lockwood has great coffee to keep you going, because this place doesn't stop all day, from morning to late at night. From a delicious breakfast accompanied by some java from Belleville Brûlerie, to lunch washed down with fresh grape juice from the owners' parents' farm, and then on to supper snacks in the basement bar with their Sriracha Bloody Mary, for example. The staff is always friendly; the crowd is always cool. Plus, the small rooms off the hall of the bar can be reserved in advance and are a great place to host your own party.

POUR VOS BEAUX YEUX

Eyewear unlike any other

10 Passage Grand Cerf (75002) / +33 1 42 36 06 79
pourvosbeauxyeux.com / Closed Sunday and lunchtime

It took me a while to figure out why Paris has so many stores selling spectacles, but apparently everyone's glasses are subsidized by the French healthcare system, so it's essentially their birthright to sport great designer eyewear. Amongst all the options though, I promise you'll find no other like Pour Vos Beaux Yeux. Their impeccably sourced vintage stock features the likes of Dior, Chanel, YSL, Balenciaga and Persol from decades past that you'll be hard pressed to find elsewhere. Each drawer is organized by brand and decade, and the friendly staff is always happy for you to try as many pairs as you like until you find that something to complement your beaux yeux.

SQUAT 59 RIVOLI

Empire of artists

59 Rue de Rivoli (75001) / +33 1 44 61 08 31
59rivoli-eng.org/main.html / Closed Monday

Midway down this commercial street, Squat 59 Rivoli brings a little
bit of raw counterculture into the mix. The seven-story, rainbow-
bannered building has been taken over by various artists and is open
(for free) to the public to experience art in progress six afternoons
a week. Inside, you can chat to sculptors, watch painters at work
and marvel at the illustrators as they sketch away. The artists each
decorate their atelier spaces as they please, and once you've perused
them all and reached the top, you can take in a spectacular view from
the balconies on the seventh floor.

perfumeries

Olfactory experiences with artisans

LIQUIDES
9 Rue de Normandie (75003), +33 9 66 94 77 06
liquides-parfums.com/en, closed Sunday

NOSE
20 Rue Bachaumont (75002), +33 1 40 26 46 03
nose.fr/en, closed Sunday

OFFICINE UNIVERSELLE BULY 1803
6 Rue Bonaparte (75006), +33 1 43 29 02 50
buly1803.com/en, closed Sunday

SERGE LUTENS
142 Galerie de Valois (75001), +33 1 49 27 09 09
en.sergelutens.com, closed Sunday

SERGE LUTENS

One doesn't need to get very close to a French person to sniff out that fragrance is a bit of an obsession for them. Luckily some fabulous perfumeries are saving us from the generic scents of overly popular colognes that shall not be named.

At **Nose**, they'll help you discover your next perfect perfume through an intense nosing session. Eventually you'll find something you love from their wide range and leave freshly fragranced. Another great selection can be found at **Liquides** in the Marais; the handsome black and brass interior holds an incredibly refined collection from independent perfume houses as well as some lesser-known classics.

At **Officine Universelle Buly 1803**, everything is done à l'ancienne, as it was when the brand was created over 200 years ago. Shopping here among the gorgeous wooden and glass shelves is as close as it gets to traveling back to the era of Belle Epoque. All the perfumes are alcohol- and glycerin-free, and are presented in glass bottles with watercolored labels.

But if there is one I trust with my scent more than anyone, it's **Serge Lutens**. This pioneer of luxury in the Palais Royal sells a special range of perfumes named after the magnificent home of his shop and available exclusively there. His Rahat Lokhum fragrance is my all-time favorite to wear.

concorde and opéra

This prestigious neighborhood sparkles with luxury and monumental Parisian architecture, from the fountains at Place de La Concorde, to landmarks such as the Obelisk at Place Vendôme, the grand columns of La Madeleine, and the ornate Opéra Garnier. There's a stellar lineup of five-star hotels along the Rue de Rivoli, and enough fine jewelry shops at Place Vendôme to satisfy their clientele. Its best shopping street however is the Rue Saint-Honoré, where fashion flagships line up to tempt you one after the other. In the south, the Jardin des Tuileries is one of the area's biggest draws, stretched between the Louvre to the east and Place de La Concorde in the west. You'll find a giant Ferris wheel in the park in summer or just next to it at Concorde during the Christmas holidays. During Fashion Week, it's a great people-watching spot, as photographers race to snap off-duty models and fashion editors leaving the shows held here. This is a glamorous neighborhood that is both a playground and runway for the international elite.

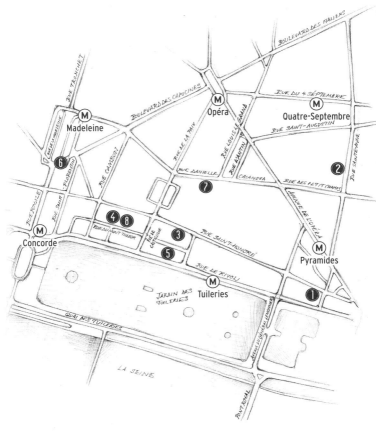

1 Astier de Villatte
2 Epices Roellinger
3 Fifi Chachnil
4 Le Soufflé

5 Librairie Galignani
6 Maille
7 Nina's Paris
8 White Bird

ASTIER DE VILLATTE

Master ceramicists

173 Rue Saint-Honoré (75001) / +33 1 42 60 74 13
astierdevillatte.com / Closed Sunday

In 2000, Ivan Pericoli and Benoît Astier de Villatte saved a little shop
on the Rue Saint-Honoré from imminent ruin. Preserving as much
as they could of its original design, they filled it with their signature
white ceramic creations. Each of their pieces, from cake stands to
plates and pots, is conceptualized in their Paris atelier and handmade
by French and Tibetan artisans. They have expanded their range to
include candles with simple but satisfying scents created with virtuoso
perfumer Françoise Caron, and introduced an array of individualized,
colorful notebooks.

EPICES ROELLINGER

All spices

51 bis Rue Sainte-Anne (75002) / +33 1 42 60 46 88
epices-roellinger.com / Closed Sunday and Monday

Within the walls of Epices Roellinger, one can travel the world through smell and taste. The owner and his wife are passionate about spices, voyaging across the globe to source a huge variety to sell in their shop. Anything you're looking for to spice up your life can be found here. Their original blended powders are some of the most magical concoctions to entertain your palate, in case you're looking for a little culinary inspiration. Infused with salts, oils, condiments and sweets as well, this space is bursting at the seams with flavor. If you can't decide what to choose, I'd say don't leave without the vanilla beans.

FIFI CHACHNIL

Lovely unmentionables

231 Rue Saint-Honoré (75001) / +33 1 42 61 21 83
fifichachnil.com/en / Closed Sunday

I fell in love with Fifi Chachnil back in California. I worked in a small lingerie shop and the buyer came home from Paris with some French underthings from Fifi's boutique. It was love at first sight. Her pastel silks and chiffons with vintage fits know how to flatter and support a real woman's body. Nowhere is Fifi's world of inspiration more evident than in her Rue Saint-Honoré shop with its boudoir décor. Tucked away off the street, it's private and girly, and the staff is always happy for you to embrace your feminine side trying on marabou trimmed robes, silk corsets and ruffled knickers. Whenever I'm in need of something pretty, Fifi is my first stop.

LE SOUFFLÉ

A French specialty

36 Rue du Mont-Thabor (75001) / +33 1 42 60 27 19
lesouffle.fr / Closed Sunday

A dish I just can't manage to get right in my own kitchen is a soufflé, of any kind, ever. Luckily for me there is Le Soufflé, the specialists of this fine French creation. Their menu of savory soufflés covers pretty much any taste your heart may desire — think traditional cheese, spinach, chicken and ham, among others. When it comes to the sweet versions, you could go for that classic Grand Marnier, which the waiter will always suggest; the luxurious chocolate version; or try out my personal recommendation, a pink pillow of deliciousness known as Le Soufflé aux Fruits Rouges.

LIBRAIRIE GALIGNANI

Elegant books

224 Rue de Rivoli (75001) / +33 1 42 60 76 07
galignani.fr/histoire-de-la-librairie-galignani.php / Closed Sunday

Despite its Franco-Italian sounding name, Librairie Galignani is proud to claim that it was the first ever English literature bookshop in continental Europe. The plaque at the front door serves as reminder, lest you forget. Contained within is Paris's most expansive collection of English writing, including the greats like Wordsworth, Byron and Thackeray, whose work the Galignani family also published in the 1800s. The store is still owned by the descendents of its founder, William, and has been in business right here since 1856. Alongside its rich history, today it has a very modern appeal with glossy art and fashion books that always draw me inside.

MAILLE

Mustard heaven

6 Place de la Madeleine (75008) / +33 1 40 15 06 00
maille.co.uk/home.dept / Closed Sunday

While the mustard capital of Dijon may be a few hundred kilometers away, Maille is stocking an impressive array of this beloved condiment at their Madeleine boutique. Among their offerings you'll find options from mustard with Chablis to one with Chardonnay, and my personal pick, black truffle. It's not everywhere you can order mustard to your liking and have it served to you in quaint antique-style jars. If watching the whole process is not enough to make you want a sandwich, then you should know there's a lot more here to make that sarnie scrumptious, like dainty little French cornichons (pickles), and seasoned oils and vinegars.

NINA'S PARIS

A royal cup of tea

29 Rue Danielle Casanova (75001) / +33 1 55 04 80 55
ninasparis.com/en/world.html / Closed Saturday and Sunday

Looking for a girly spot to get the Marie Antoinette experience without making the trip out to Versailles? Then drop into Nina's Paris near Place Vendôme. This tiny little tea place is pretty in pink and ultra sweet thanks to their special almond cake with fondant icing. Their Marie Antoinette brew is a black tea with a fruity and floral essence. In fact it's flavored with apples from the King's kitchen garden at Versailles. You can sip it in tranquility at one of the several tables in the tea room (no Ladurée-style crowds here) or stock up on their royal blend so you can live like a queen and drink it back at home.

WHITE BIRD

Eclectic jewelry purveyor

38 Rue du Mont-Thabor (75001) / +33 1 58 62 25 86
whitebirdjewellery.com / Closed Sunday

Place Vendôme is lined with luxury jewelry brands like Chopard, Dior and Tiffany, but a mere hop and a skip away is an equally dazzling and more eclectic alternative on Rue du Mont-Thabor. White Bird carries a range of small independent designers from Paris and beyond. Stéphanie, the owner and resident purveyor of fine, pretty jewels, spent most of her career working in jewelry and watches for French fashion houses before opening her dream shop. Her simple and delicate selection of rings, necklaces, bracelets and other baubles is a superb option for the modern woman who prefers clean silhouettes and subtle accessorizing.

pigalle and montmartre

In recent years there has been an exciting revival of these somewhat gritty neighborhoods in the north of Paris, particularly Pigalle. The trendy South Pigalle district, or So-Pi as it's being called these days, is better known now for its hipster bars and good eats than for its sex shops. Some people complain that the gentrification of the area detracts from its authenticity, but if the smartening up means gourmet groceries, great coffee and good shopping, then I'm all for it. Walk up the Rue des Martyrs and you'll pass many of the neighborhood's highlights. Just north of Pigalle, the hill becomes Montmartre, made famous by the quirky film *Amélie* and the artists who over the years chose this elevated village as home. The Sacré Coeur boasts one of the most stunning views of the city, and by following tips on the quaint winding cobblestone streets around it, you can avoid most of the tourist traps on the main square to find some real gems.

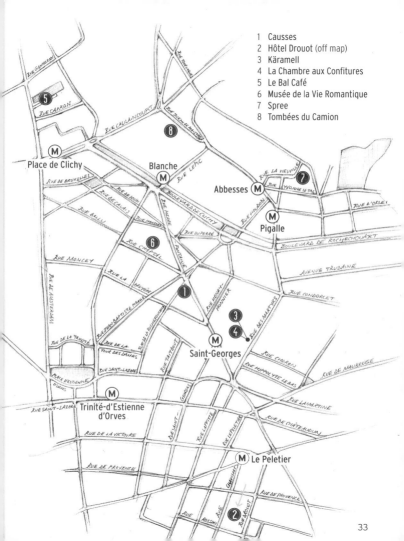

1 Causses
2 Hôtel Drouot (off map)
3 Käramell
4 La Chambre aux Confitures
5 Le Bal Café
6 Musée de la Vie Romantique
7 Spree
8 Tombées du Camion

Place de Clichy
Blanche
Abbesses
Pigalle
Saint-Georges
Trinité-d'Estienne d'Orves
Le Peletier

33

CAUSSES

Upmarket groceries

55 Rue Notre-Dame de Lorette (75009) / +33 1 53 16 10 10
causses.org / Closed Saturday and Sunday

I love living in the Marais, but my only regret is that it's rather impractical to do my food shopping at my favorite store in South Pigalle, Causses. Nothing quite inspires me to cook like exploring their alimentation général. The consistent quality of their produce is hard to beat, and there are always discoveries to be made as they stock an assortment of rare vegetables and fruits like topinambours (Jerusalem artichokes) and Chioggia beets, for example. Working with mostly niche French suppliers, their cheeses, meats and more are exceptional. Maybe you need some help figuring out how to cook up all the gourmet grub back at home? Easy: just sign up for one of their cooking classes.

HÔTEL DROUOT

Auctions every day

9 Rue Drouot (75009) / +33 1 48 00 20 20 / drouot.com
Closed Sunday

I spent several years working in antiques before moving to Paris, and eventually made friends with a few dealers here. One showed me the Hôtel Drouot one day, which, unusually for Paris, runs auctions nearly daily. Depending on the type of sale, you can rummage through old collectibles, flip through dusty books, watch bidders go after famous art, pick out furniture, or marvel at fine jewelry. But if you're a serious shopper, be warned: you'll be competing with antique and art dealers, and phone-bidders worldwide. I mostly go just to see what ends up here, and how much people will pay to take it home.

KÄRAMELL

Swedish treats

15 Rue des Martyrs (75009) / +33 1 53 21 91 77 / karamell.fr
Open daily

I thought I had outgrown my candy crazed years, but then I found myself leaving Käramell one day with a pink and white striped bag weighing over a pound. This funky little shop founded by Lena, originally from the south of Sweden, sells sweets from her homeland in every conceivable shape, color and flavor. American candy with its high fructose corn syrup holds no candle to these bonbons, as from what I now understand the Swedes take their confectionery as seriously as the French take their wine. Real Swedish Fish are just the start of things at the candy bar with gummies and chocolate in irresistible cute shapes, as well as salty black licorice, which is a specialty here.

LA CHAMBRE AUX CONFITURES

For jam lovers only

9 Rue des Martyrs (75009) / +33 1 71 73 43 77
lachambreauxconfitures.com / Closed Sunday

I sometimes look back on my life in America before moving to Paris and think "I can't believe we used to serve jam with a knife!" In France, with jam (confiture in French), as with butter, there is no need for moderation. Get out the spoon, and help yourself to a generous serving because there is plenty to go around here. In fact, they'll even sell you a spoon along with your jar here to encourage such excess. Just a few of their flavors your toast could desire are Champagne peach, apricot lavender and cherry mint. Owner Lise started her boutique because she always loved jams. She works with chefs around the country and will guide you through her dozens of jams, chutneys and marmalades asking questions like a perfumer until you find the exact combination that most tickles your taste buds.

FRIPONNES

LE BAL CAFÉ

Neo-bistrot for brunch and lunch

6 Impasse de la Défense (75018) / +33 1 44 70 75 50
le-bal.fr / Closed Monday and Tuesday

Not many tourists would find themselves here at Place de Clichy, but being surprisingly close to Montmartre and the Sacré Coeur, it is well worth the quick walk to dine at this café annex to Le Bal Gallery. The chefs hail from the delectable and famous Rose Bakery, not far away on the Rue des Martyrs. They've brought with them their mix of hearty French and British cuisine and have thrown in some great coffee with a master barista. A classic brunch of bacon, eggs, tomato and toast is a great way to kick-start a day in Montmartre, or you could polish off an afternoon by stopping in for some scones with jam and a cup of tea.

MUSÉE DE LA VIE ROMANTIQUE

Romance reborn

16 Rue Chaptal (75009) / +33 1 55 31 95 67
paris.fr/pratique/musees-expos/musee-de-la-vie-romantique/p5851
Closed Monday

I moved to Paris in search of a romantic life. Each time I visit this pink and green townhouse at the foot of Montmartre, I'm certain I've found it. The museum was once home to artist Ary Scheffer, who spent his life here painting when he wasn't busy with friends like Frédéric Chopin, George Sand and Charles Dickens visiting. It's as if the walls could tell stories of their composing, painting and writing. Downstairs is a collection of mementos and watercolors by George Sand herself, and throughout the rest of the property are artworks accumulated over the years. I love to visit in spring to enjoy tea on the terrace while imagining what it would have been like to live here.

SPREE

Art meets fashion

16 Rue la Vieuville (75018) / +33 1 42 23 41 40 / spree.fr
Closed Monday and Sunday mornings

In my opinion, Spree is Montmartre's most stylish shop, perfectly embodying the life of the chic Parisian woman who would call this artsy neighborhood home. Exploring the relationship between fashion and art, the space is filled with a mix of mid-century modern furniture and unique home décor items at the front, and an on-point selection of clothing at the rear. Isabel Marant Étoile, Cedric Charlier and Comme des Garçons are some of the labels featured here, along with up-and-coming designers that co-owner Roberta has a knack for discovering. You can also visit her husband across the street, heading up the rotating exhibitions at their gallery.

TOMBÉES DU CAMION

One Parisian's trash is another's treasure

17 Rue Joseph de Maistre (75018) / +33 9 81 21 62 80
tombeesducamion.com / Open daily

The name of this little shop in Montmartre loosely translates as "what fell off the truck." That's pretty much what you get here, and it's a lot of fun sorting through the mix of knickknacks sourced from dead stock in abandoned factories throughout France. You never know what you might happen upon that you may find inspiring or even quite useful. Retro toys, antique glass vials, faded postcards, vintage clothing labels, keychains, buttons, patches, locks, stamps and so much more are all up for grabs in the surprisingly very well organized shop that will make you feel like a kid again.

BOOT CAFÉ
19 Rue du Pont aux Choux (75004), +33 6 26 41 10 66
facebook.com/bootcafe, open daily

COUTUME CAFÉ
47 Rue de Babylone (75007), +33 1 45 51 50 47
coutumecafe.com, open daily

FONDATION CAFÉ
16 Rue Dupetit Thouars (75003), no phone
facebook.com/fondationcafe, open daily

KB CAFÉSHOP
53 Avenue Trudaine (75009), +33 1 56 92 12 41
facebook.com/CafeShopSouthPigalle, open daily

LA CAFÉOTHÈQUE
52 Rue de l'Hôtel-de-Ville (75004), +33 1 53 01 83 84
lacafeotheque.com/en, open daily

TEN BELLES
10 Rue de la Grange aux Belles (75010), +33 1 42 40 90 78
tenbelles.com, open daily

coffee break

Sip on the city's best brews

Considering the generous amount of time the average Parisian is willing to put aside for a caffeine break, the French capital was oddly lacking in quality coffee houses until fairly recently. But now, thanks to the return of some stellar French baristas bringing their knowledge home, and the arrival of a few foreigners, robust brews are available all over town.

On the Right Bank, **La Caféothèque** was among the first in the city to step up the game. Just writing the name makes me smell the tantalizing aroma of freshly ground espresso beans. On the Left Bank, the French and Australian duo behind **Coutume Café** pioneered sophisticated coffee science in Paris. The décor is simple, but once you notice the elaborate brewing machine, you'll see the beverage-making process is not.

KB Caféshop in South Pigalle is my go-to place to fuel up sufficiently to make it up the steep hill to Montmartre. The occasional sign outside **Ten Belles** proclaiming "Drinking good coffee is sexy" is a calling card for trendies, who can fill up the narrow café rather quickly. The good news is that Canal Saint-Martin about 10 steps away is just the right place to enjoy their java to go. A little south from there, **Fondation Café** is serious about its coffee but never pretentious, always imparting a bit of knowledge to those eager to learn. The tiny **Boot Café** still has the original façade of its predecessor, a shoe repair shop, and if you pause to admire it, the friendly barista will be sure to wave you inside to taste the coffee.

strasbourg – saint-denis

canal saint-martin

Once upon a time, the Gare de l'Est and Gare du Nord train stations were the main reasons for venturing this way. For a while now, though, Paris's 10th arrondissement has been on its way up. The double arches at the meeting of Rue Saint-Martin and Grands Boulevards mark the threshold of what is now a hipster haven of sorts. Between its African salons, Arab boucheries and Asian nail salons, a vibrant mélange of cultures converges here during the day. At night, the restaurants are where all the action is and the area's slightly more affordable rents mean that there are plenty of locals to keep them busy. Further east, you'll arrive at the Canal Saint-Martin with its picturesque bridges. The canal reaches its full potential at the height of summer with picnickers along its banks day and night, but year round, here are many of the neighborhood's most beloved spots to drink and dine. Duck into the little side streets and there is plenty to discover as well. More so each year as this corner of Paris becomes increasingly magnetic for young entrepreneurs.

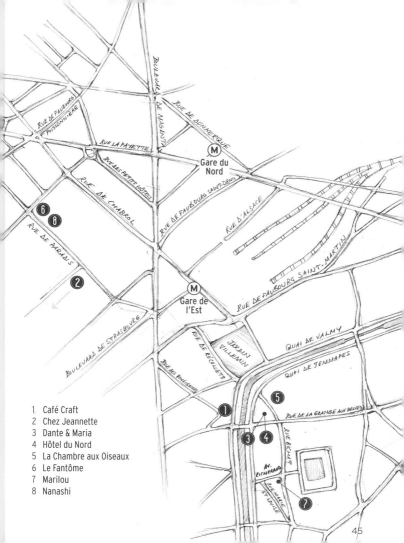

1. Café Craft
2. Chez Jeannette
3. Dante & Maria
4. Hôtel du Nord
5. La Chambre aux Oiseaux
6. Le Fantôme
7. Marilou
8. Nanashi

45

CAFÉ CRAFT

Working lunch

24 Rue des Vinaigriers (75010) / +33 1 40 35 90 77
cafe-craft.com / Open daily

One thing I appreciate about the French is their laissez-faire attitude to you sitting for hours on end in their cafés dragging out an espresso. However, those teeny tables aren't so conducive to a bit of work, and their attitude isn't so charming when you pull out a 21st-century laptop in their charming early 20th-century eatery. As a freelancer, I struggled with that until I found Café Craft. This work-friendly coffee haven has free Wi-Fi and a spacious communal desk with plenty of plugs to keep your batteries charged. I don't recommend wasting your precious time in Paris working, but if you have to, Café Craft is a nice compromise. I'll be happy to share the desk there with you.

CHEZ JEANNETTE

Long live the French bistrot

47 Rue du Faubourg Saint-Denis (75010) / +33 1 47 70 30 89
chezjeannette.com / Open daily

Rescued from ruin and its original owner, Jeannette, a stylish young crew took over this joint several years back and cleaned it up. They chose to forgo the temptation to turn it into another Brooklyn-inspired outpost (Paris has too many of those now, if you ask me) and instead managed to improve on its quintessential Parisian-ness. It's now a popular place for "un after-work" (said with a strong French accent), which in Paris is yuppy slang for good drinks, plenty of food and some handsome strangers to strike up a conversation with. You'll find all of the above at Chez Jeannette.

DANTE & MARIA

Sweet and sassy accessories

3 Rue de la Grange aux Belles (75010) / +33 1 70 22 62 13
dantemaria.fr / Closed Sunday and Monday

Just off the Canal Saint-Martin, this sassy little boudoir-esque boutique looks like an adult dollhouse and stocks dainty jewelry designed by its owner, Karine. She named the shop after her grandparents, from whom she inherited her love of trinkets. It all sounds very sweet until you take a closer look. Her affordable accessories are created with the idea of changing them based on your mood. "Love" and "Hate" rings can be swapped according to how your day is going, a star pendant with the f-word scribbled across is both nice and naughty, or a silver charm reading "Non, non, et non" lets people know you mean business. In addition to jewelry, clever and cute needlepoint of the same humorous nature is available too.

HÔTEL DU NORD

Bohemian lunch, swanky dinner

102 Quai de Jemmapes (75010) / +33 1 40 40 78 78
hoteldunord.org / Open daily

Don't be confused by the name: the Hôtel du Nord is not a place to sleep at, but to eat. It's named after the French film of the same title and its cinematic inspiration appears on the walls in the form of framed old movie posters. In the evening, the flickering candles and white tablecloths exude a chic elegance. The corner lounge and sofa area is ideal for cuddling up to a date and relaxing before or after dinner with a drink. For carnivores, the menu here can't be beat with classic French dishes such as confit de canard and beef bourguignon getting modern updates with market fresh accompaniments.

LA CHAMBRE AUX OISEAUX

Relaxed brunch off the canal

48 Rue Bichat (75010) / +33 1 40 18 98 49
lachambreauxoiseaux.fr / Closed Monday and Tuesday

A mix of Art Deco, Art Nouveau and a bit of shabby chic, this café is a recreation of the childhood bedroom of its co-founder, Léna. Her partner Hervé has always been passionate about both cuisine and décor, and could never decide between the two. When the pair met, they brought their mutual love of both together by opening La Chambre aux Oiseaux. Antique porcelain, mixed floral motifs and heirlooms from each of their families decorate the space, giving it a homey vibe for an excellent brunch near the Canal Saint-Martin. Their triple-decker club sandwich and sweet treats are more than enough to ensure you don't leave hungry.

LE FANTÔME

Boozy arcade with gourmet snacks

36 Rue de Paradis (75010) / +33 9 66 87 11 20 / lefantome.fr
Closed Sunday

Confession... I'm not a heavy drinker and I'm a touch irked that it sometimes feels like the only nocturnal social activity in Paris. I'm glad that Le Fantôme has thrown a nice option into the mix for a friendly rendezvous to take place. Take a bar, add a bunch of retro arcade games and offer pizza – I'm pretty set to hang out all night. This is the cool new kid amongst the evening haunts in the 10th that is filled with a bunch of, well, cool kids. It may sound like an average arcade, but gourmet food and quality cocktails prove everything is better in Paris. Now excuse me while I go get in line for Pac-Man...

MARILOU

Sharing is caring

8 Rue Marie et Louise (75010) / +33 1 71 20 96 67
restaurantmarilou.com / Closed Sunday

A wonderful place to come with friends, Marilou's delicious plates
are intended for family-style dining. It's a good thing they're small
though, because to choose just one or two would be impossible for me.
In fact, sometimes I just order them all. Roasted stuffed figs wrapped
in prosciutto, gooey burrata and tomatoes, pistachio-crusted chicken
strips with spicy dipping sauce, eggplant and ricotta... I can't stop
myself here. Inevitably the whole menu will end up on our table, but
the idea is to share so I don't hog it all for myself. If you do end up
having a little more than expected, the nearby Canal Saint-Martin is
the perfect place to walk it off.

NANASHI

The Parisian bento

**31 Rue de Paradis (75010) / +33 1 40 22 05 55 / nanashi.fr
Open daily**

Despite the distance between their two countries, there is a synergy and mutual admiration between the French and Japanese in art, fashion and food. Nowhere is this more tastily evident than at Nanashi, where they have created the Parisian bento, among many other Franco-Japanese concoctions. Special daily vegetable and meat bentos are best drenched in Asian barbecue sauce and topped with tons of sesame seeds and umami seasonings. Matcha lovers will also be quite happy to find a range of desserts and drinks here with this star ingredient. Whenever I'm in the mood for some healthy and flavorful grub, Nanashi is a great spot to chow down.

PARIS AFTER DARK:
hidden treasures

Tucked away nightlife gems in the City of Light

Never having taken to the American sports bars of my West Coast home town, I was a nightlife novice when I moved to Paris. It took me a while to uncover places I liked as the city's top joints are also some of its most inconspicuous.

Le Magnifique was my introduction to the finer side of nightlife. Ring the doorbell to get the doorman's attention and if you pass the dress code, inside you'll find a gorgeous bar lined with roses and plush, dimly lit seating. This is somewhere you can enjoy drinking your Piscine in privacy.

A couple of years ago a much needed dose of nightlife for a bourgeois neighborhood increasingly intolerant of nocturnal noise arrived in the form of **Little Red Door** in the Marais. Perhaps the locals haven't caught on yet that some of the city's finest cocktails are now being served at their stoop.

LE CARMEN
34 Rue Duperré (75009), +33 1 45 26 50 00
le-carmen.fr, open daily

LE MAGNIFIQUE
25 Rue de Richelieu (75001), +33 1 42 60 70 80
emagnifique.fr, open daily

LITTLE RED DOOR
60 Rue Charlot (75003), +33 1 42 71 19 32
lrdparis.com, open daily

MOONSHINER
5 Rue Sedaine (75011), +33 9 50 73 12 99
facebook.com/pages/Moonshiner/390791131035525
open daily

SILENCIO
142 Rue Montmartre (75002), +33 1 40 13 12 33
silencio-club.com/en, closed Sunday and Monday

THE BEEF CLUB
58 Rue Jean-Jacques Rousseau (75001)
+33 9 54 37 13 65, fr-ca.facebook.com/
LeBallroomDuBeefclub, closed Sunday

The first time I made it to **Moonshiner**, I was convinced I had totally screwed up on the address. I found myself at a place called Pizza De Vito, and was directed toward the refrigerator. Reluctantly, I entered and was transported to what has become one of my favorite bars in town. It's a similar story at **The Beef Club**, which is the perfect place to dine and then hit their "ballroom" hidden beneath. I like to end the night here with a Morning Glory Scotch Fizz.

Le Carmen was once home to the opera composer Georges Bizet and its façade means it could still easily be mistaken for someone's private residence. But inside its Rococo interior is one of my most-loved clubs for great music and dancing. For those extra late nights, if you pass a dapper doorman on the Rue Montmartre, you're likely to have found **Silencio**. Deep down its winding staircase is the bar designed by David Lynch, and drinks to rival the amazing décor.

les bars à vins

The taste of France by the bottle or glass

FRENCHIE BAR À VINS
5-6 Rue du Nil (75002), +33 1 40 39 96 19
frenchie-restaurant.com/en, closed Saturday and Sunday

LA BUVETTE
67 Rue Saint-Maur (75011), +33 9 83 56 94 11
no website, closed Monday and Tuesday

Ô CHATEAU
68 Rue Jean-Jacques Rousseau (75001), +33 1 44 73 97 80
o-chateau.com, closed Sunday

VERJUS BAR À VINS
47 Rue de Montpensier (75001), +33 1 42 97 54 40
verjusparis.com/fr-bar-a-vins
closed Saturday and Sunday

Ô CHATEAU

Wine is an unbeatable way to imbibe some French culture and time in Paris wouldn't be well spent without enjoying some quintessential bars à vins. At the award-winning **Ô Chateau**, there are 40 wines by the glass and hundreds by the bottle, which is a good thing because I return frequently and never get bored.

After some of the city's top restaurants became so popular it's impossible to get a reservation even two weeks out, the chefs did us a favor and opened up no-reservation bars next door. Such is the case with **Frenchie's** and **Verjus' bar à vins**, both of which boast eclectic bottle lists from

VERJUS' BAR À VINS

producers who are as mad about wine as the chefs are about cuisine.
They don't let us go hungry though; they also offer mouthwatering
spin-offs of their finest dishes to pair with your vino of choice.

For the personal touch, the one-woman show at the teeny
La Buvette provides an in-depth introduction to carefully selected wines.
A bit of her paté, terrine or saucissons is the ideal complement to whatever
you choose for your glass.

oberkampf and belleville

In recent years, the allure of the Marais has slowly but surely overflowed its borders, bringing some of Paris's leading designers and eateries to the once less exciting Boulevard Beaumarchais. The street is now the hip address for stylish flagships. Heading up Rue Oberkampf leads you into the heart of what I'd say has become the tastiest quarter of Paris. The city's most established and up-and-coming chefs have flocked here and populated it with some of the hottest tables in town. The modern French cuisine and organic wine menus offered by many of them appeal to the discerning international food crowd and the restaurants quickly fill up. Also for those cosmopolitan tourists who have caught on that this is the place to be, a handful of old industrial buildings have been renovated into cool hotels where they can rest their party-weary heads. Further east, in Belleville, there are a number of great music venues from where performers and audiences feed into the local bars when the show is over.

1 À Boire et à Manger (off map)
2 Au Passage
3 Aux Deux Amis
4 L'Échappée
5 Le Dauphin
6 Le Kitch
7 Le Servan
8 Les Niçois
9 Les Trois 8
10 Musée Edith Piaf
11 Nail Club

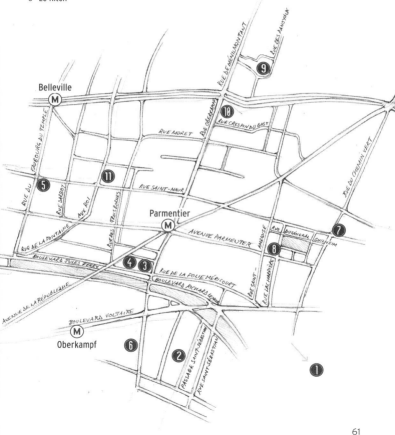

À BOIRE ET À MANGER

Cute and yummy

61 Rue Oberkampf (75011) / +33 1 43 38 11 03
facebook.com/aboireetamanger / Closed Monday

If I'm looking for something special to snack on, À Boire et à Manger with its picturesque white and black striped awning is just the answer. This little gourmet grocer stocks a very tempting array of specialties you won't find at the average Paris épicerie, like scoops of fresh almonds and walnuts and a huge selection of chocolates in flavors such as pepper rose and masala chai. I always stock up on truffle salt from their condiment, jam and spice shelves. In the fridge are real lemonades, juices and natural sodas, and there's the usual French greatness of a fine assortment of wines and cheeses. If you can't wait to get home to snack on your shopping, you can also order a fresh sandwich. This is the grocery store to wish for in your own neighborhood.

AU PASSAGE

French tapas and wine bar

1 Bis Passage Saint-Sébastien (75011) / +33 1 43 55 07 52
aupassage.com / Closed Sunday

Some friends and I had the pleasure of meeting the then unknown chef from Au Passage at a local bar. He invited us back for a little tasting and some great wine. It was the best midnight snack I've ever had, so it makes sense that Au Passage and its original chef, James Henry, are now a huge success. Henry has since moved on to new culinary endeavors, but the food here hasn't suffered one bit. From raw scallops with basil oil and edible flowers, to roasted cauliflower with spicy aioli sauce, to white chocolate ice cream with a bit of crumble, every course is an absolute delight, never over done and always just right.

AUX DEUX AMIS

Natural wines and unnaturally good small dishes

45 Rue Oberkampf (75011) / +33 1 58 30 38 13
facebook.com/Aux-Deux-Amis / Closed Sunday and Monday

The crowd at this jovial joint is a mixed bag of vino lovers who come for the friendly atmosphere and the long list of natural wines. By the glass or by the bottle, their selection is sourced directly from the growers and definitely has the stamp of approval of Paris's most discerning winos, who you'll always find at the bar. The food is equally exceptional, with melt-in-your-mouth prosciutto, mussels in flavorful broth, Spanish tortilla, trofie pesto and fresh fish options. Because the food and drink is top notch and very fairly priced, this small space gets packed quite quickly, so stop in early if you don't fancy waiting for a table.

L'ÉCHAPPÉE

Urban spa

64 Rue de la Folie Méricourt (75011) / +33 1 58 30 12 50
lechappee.com / Closed Tuesday

I'm not going to lie; winter in Paris can be brutal. When there've been just too many days of gray weighing me down and no plane to whisk me off to somewhere sunny and relaxing, I sneak away to L'Échappée and spoil myself at the hammam. Pilates or yoga classes are a great way to decompress, but I can't fib about this either — I'm not that sporty so I skip straight to a nice massage and make the most of the steam room and Jacuzzi afterwards. The location has an ultra clean aesthetic, which is blissful for sophisticated relaxation. They even have special pampering options for extra deserving expectant mothers.

LE DAUPHIN

Modern French cuisine and organic wines

131 Avenue Parmentier (75011) / +33 1 55 28 78 88
restaurantledauphin.net / Closed Sunday and Monday

Le Dauphin is the chic younger brother and neighbor of the renowned Chateaubriand, so when it opened we all knew we had to try it. Just as at Chateaubriand, the bottle list is all organic, and many people try to call Le Dauphin their wine bar. I think that's selling it short, though, because the food here is out of this world. Like many of Paris's foremost restaurants in recent years, the focus is on eating several small plates that are incredibly inventive, such as tandoori octopus, tuna tartare with raspberries and almonds, or cream of corn and coffee. The other thing I'm in love with here is its floor-to-ceiling Carrara marble interior, which is absolutely stunning.

LE KITCH

Quirky cocktails

10 Rue Oberkampf (75011) / +33 1 40 21 94 41
facebook.com/pages/Le-Kitch / Open daily

An eccentric little dive bar, Le Kitch is very dear to my heart after many
great nights spent sipping on their infamous "Shrek" cocktail — the
house specialty, and a refreshing blended mix of mint, lemon and gin.
"Kitch" is definitely the way to describe the place, illuminated year
round in twinkling lights, with mismatched tables beneath a cloud-
painted ceiling of flying pigs and a disco ball overhead. With found
objects such as garden gnomes and pink Eiffel Towers decorating the
shelves behind the bar, nothing about this place is very refined. It's fun
and friendly, and that is just what we all need by Friday night, when I
usually head here.

LE SERVAN

French cooking with flair

32 Rue Saint-Maur (75011) / +33 1 55 28 51 82 / leservan.com
Closed Saturday and Sunday

If there's one guy I trust with recommendations of where to eat in
Paris, it's my fellow American David Lebovitz. It's thanks to him I
found Le Servan. This corner bistrot looks rather simple initially, but
once inside, look up and notice its beautiful hand-painted ceiling and
crown moldings. But you came for the food, so here is what you'll get —
delicious seasonally driven cuisine prepared with international flair and
priced reasonably. The chef is part French, part Filipino, and not afraid to
bring uncommon spices to her cuisine. The secret here seems to be in
the sauces, like the spicy apricot and tangy green herb concoctions that
make dishes even more succulent than they already are.

LES NIÇOIS

Pétanque bar

7 Rue Lacharrière (75011) / +33 9 84 16 55 03 / lesnicois.com
Closed Monday

Les Niçois brings the spirit of the South of France to Paris. It's a great spot, right on the enchanting Square Gardette, to spend a few hours eating, drinking and playing pétanque, which are of course the three favored pastimes of our countrymen from Toulouse to Nice. The pétanque takes place in the basement. You might think it would be good to start down there, seeing as after a healthy amount of their great wines or beers on tap, you won't be throwing straight. But if you really want to do as Les Niçois do, hit the bar first and don't forget the snacks. Their small plates like chickpea fritters and croquettes, for example, are perfect for sharing with friends before you challenge them to a round downstairs.

LES TROIS 8

Top-notch beers

11 Rue Victor Letalle (75020) / +33 1 40 33 47 70 / lestrois8.fr
Open daily

I discovered this local thanks to a long-time friend originally from Colorado. In the Rockies, crafting beer is a way of life, so naturally she of all people led me here. Les Trois 8 serves French and European artisanal beers, bottled and on tap, at very affordable prices, and each draft brew is served in the glass of its maker. The menu changes weekly, as you'll notice from the chalkboard listing. The décor is no frills and fuss, much like the casual and young neighborhood you'll find it in. Even though beer is kind of a guy thing in France, the rose hibiscus blanche is awfully feminine and my personal choice. And if you do insist on being a wino when in France, they've got great organic wines as well.

MUSÉE ÉDITH PIAF

Life and times of the French songstress

5 Rue Crespin du Gast (75011) / +33 1 43 55 52 72 / No website
Open Monday through Wednesday

Before she became one of the most beloved song birds of all time, Édith Piaf was just an orphan singing on the streets of Belleville, Paris's 20th arrondissement. Today you can find the little-known Musée de Édith Piaf in the same neighborhood, created and maintained by a small foundation, Les Amis de Piaf. The intimate museum is one of the tenderest displays of fan affection, taking up two rooms of Bernard Marchois' apartment and filled with mementos, photographs, clothing and information from the singer's fascinating life. Bernard opens the museum to everyone for free, but donations are greatly appreciated.

NAIL CLUB
Cute manicure collective

134 Rue Saint-Maur (75011) / +33 9 82 51 33 75 / nailclub.fr
Closed Sunday and Monday

Nail art hasn't quite taken off in France as it has elsewhere, but as a beauty junkie myself, I would like to see it imported here more. Perhaps it's because French women, despite their reputation for being beauty experts, rarely go for a professional manicure. Nonetheless, the fun and creative girls that make up Nail Club in the 11th arrondissement are extending style to the fingertips of the city's fashionistas one hand at a time. They create original nail art (or bring your own ideas) and also sell a great collection of lesser-known polishes and other nail care products. They'll even teach you how to create your own nail art with their expert tutorials and prepare take-home kits containing everything you need.

rainy day hideaways

Stay dry exploring Paris's great indoors

CINÉMA DU PANTHÉON
13 Rue Victor Cousin (75005), +33 1 40 46 01 21
whynotproductions.fr/pantheon, open daily

LA GRANDE PRAIRIE
19–21 Rue Boyer (75020), +33 1 46 36 07 07, labellevilloise.
com/category/evenements/espace/la-grande-prairie
closed Monday and Tuesday

LE 104
5 Rue Curial (75019), +33 1 53 35 50 00, 104.fr/english
closed Monday

LE COMPTOIR GÉNÉRAL
80 Quai de Jemmapes (75010), +33 1 44 88 24 48
lecomptoirgeneral.com/en, open daily

LES FRIGOS
19 Rue des Frigos (75013), no phone
les-frigos.com, open Saturday and Sunday

PASSAGE DES PANORAMAS
11 Boulevard Montmartre (75002), no phone
passagedespanoramas.fr, open daily

Our British capital neighbor to the north, London, seems to have gotten the reputation for gray skies and drizzle. Statistically, though, Paris has about just as many such days. Don't be surprised if even in summer the clouds roll in and rain on your picnic.

You can shelter from the elements by heading indoors to **La Grande Prairie** above La Bellevilloise and sprawl out on one of the lawn chairs shielded from the showers with a bar at arm's reach. Or you can head to **Le Comptoir Général** and fantasize about warmer climes in its Franco-African atmosphere complete with a "ghetto museum", café and thrift shop.

While the rain is coming down, I'm tempted to miss America's indoor shopping malls to wait it out, but I assure you its architectural precursor, Paris's Passages, are far more quaint and charming. The indoor **Passage des Panoramas** has amazing specialty shops, cafés and galleries to keep you busy for an entire afternoon.

If you prefer to sit instead of stroll, take in a double feature at **Cinéma du Panthéon**, a landmark of French New Wave film that a philosophy scholar at the Sorbonne introduced me to in my first year in Paris. Truffaut, Godard and such will give you plenty to discuss over a drink and a snack at the coffeeshop afterwards.

Lastly, if you're a fan of the arts, at **Le 104** or **Les Frigos**, you can stay dry exploring the ateliers of tons of artists at work. Both have their own cafés, while Le 104 even has its own shops, indoor playground and always a source of amusement, a photo booth.

PASSAGE DES PANORAMAS

bastille and bercy

From Bastille to Bercy is what I call a very authentic and balanced Parisian neighborhood. Not always the most attractive or clean, it's a bit rough in the middle and polished on the edges, with the picturesque quay of the Seine bordering it to the south and the refined Marais just to its west. In the center, its rock 'n' roll heart comes to life with a string of casual bars and hipster haunts. After sundown, the charming cobble-stoned Rue de Lappe turns into a stretch of debauchery and late night crêpe stalls stand guard to feed the mass exodus from the bars at 2am. But by morning, things are back in order and the charming Rue Charonne opens up with a string of appealing shops and cafés. Just next door in the 12th arrondissement, the local inhabitants mingle at the daily market on Rue d'Aligre, where you can shop bright and early for food and flowers. Further southeast, the streets settle into a residential calm, most endearingly so on Rue Cremieux with its rainbow-colored houses.

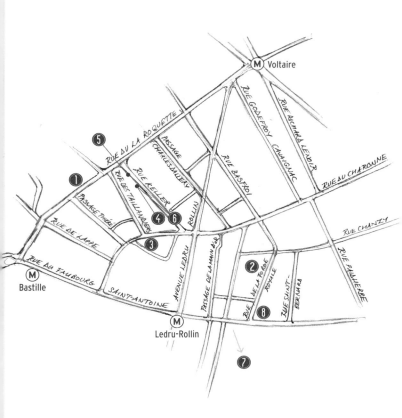

1 Adöm
2 Bloom
3 French Trotters
4 Gaëlle Barré

5 Living Room
6 Maison Aimable
7 Musée des Arts Forains (off map)
8 Red House

ADÖM

Vintage outfitters

35 Rue de la Roquette (75011) / +33 1 48 07 15 94 / No website
Open daily

One of my cherished pastimes in Paris is vintage shopping. In the US there are high-end vintage stores and then crazy disorganized thrift shops. Paris's "fripperies", on the other hand, are affordable curations of already sorted pre-loved threads ready for the find. One of the best is Adöm at Bastille, which is packed full of cool stuff but incredibly well arranged and clean. It has clothes for both men and women, and the staff is always friendly and helpful, and can converse at length about the latest treasure you pulled out from the bargain bin. If the crowds have scared you away from the famous fripperies of the neighboring Marais, this is a nice place to come and thrift in a calmer climate.

BLOOM

Local, organic and homemade

25 Rue de la Forge Royale (75011) / +33 1 43 72 87 88
bloom-restaurant.fr / Closed Monday

When it comes to the simple life, it has never tasted so lovely as at my dearest little eatery for a fresh, local and organic lunch. Owner Pauline is also the friendly waitress of her café's five colorful tables. When I'm in the mood for something home cooked, but unmotivated to cook for myself, I stroll here for a hearty meal. The menu changes daily, but on it you may find a nice pumpkin soup in autumn, vegetarian lasagne, salad with brown rice or fudge brownies. Bloom sits on a quiet street, and just in front is a tiny corner park that provides a charming view.

FRENCH TROTTERS

Cosmopolitan clothing

30 Rue de Charonne (75011) / +33 1 47 00 84 35
frenchtrotters.fr / Closed Sunday

The French Trotter is actually a breed of horse, and after some contemplating I realized the shop's name must have something to do with the owners' tendencies to giddy on over to a different city each season and bring back their favorite designers – Christophe Lemaire, Xuan-Thu Nguyen, Anna Sui and Sigerson Morrison, to name a few. Despite their international inspiration, they always manage to present a range of quintessential Parisian style. That effortless and timeless chic look, never over or under dressed, never too trendy yet never out of fashion. Oh, le sigh... I'm still trying to master that one after seven years in France, but a visit here seems a good place to start.

GAËLLE BARRÉ

A woman's world

17 Rue Keller (75011) / +33 1 43 14 63 02 / gaellebarre.com
Closed Sunday

Gaëlle Barré studied couture and opened her shop near Bastille
fresh out of school back in 1998. She has since managed to grow a
successful retail business without outgrowing her reputation as a
truly local designer. Her design sensibility perfectly demonstrates
her understanding of the Parisian women she dresses. A roomy
tweed coat with velvet pockets, a mod matching skirt and jacket,
or the ideal wrap dress are all things you might find on the racks of
her Rue Keller store. Poetic and feminine with a retro touch, they are
figure-flattering, versatile and easy to wear. Now a mom, Gaëlle has
launched a children's clothing line as well.

LIVING ROOM

The original dry cut

22 Rue des Taillandiers (75011) / +33 1 43 55 66 81
livingroomparis.com / Closed Saturday and Sunday

I recommend dry cutting for anyone who gets anxious at the hairdressers. It removes the guesswork because you can see the shape as it forms and better control the results. No surprises and no crying at Living Room, just good hair days. Its founder, Matt, was trained in London and came back to Paris eventually to open his own salon. When it comes to color, he uses only ammonia-free products enriched with grapeseed oil. With '70s hip hop playing in the background, a nice array of glossy magazines and some cool swag on display, this is the place to chill and enjoy a stress-free haircut.

MAISON AIMABLE

Gorgeous home goods

16-18 Rue des Taillandiers (75011) / +33 9 82 53 16 18
maison-aimable.com / Closed Sunday

Maison Aimable stocks all the little things that make a house a home. Their contemporary assortment of bits and bobs has a versatile aesthetic to fit many different décor sensibilities. Completing your kitchen? A selection of modern slate, marble and wooden cutting boards will serve you well. Planning on entertaining? Pretty hand-dyed linen napkins will complete a table setting. Got empty wall space? Fill it in with a beautiful brass-framed mirror. There are also succulent house plants, baskets, vases, light fixtures and many more goodies all sourced from Denmark, Japan and the UK. All in all, the shop hits a great balance of selling quality goods at affordable prices.

MUSÉE DES ARTS FORAINS

All the fun of the fair

**53 Avenue des Terroirs de France (75012) / +33 1 43 40 16 22
arts-forains.com / Open daily, by reservation**

I do realize carnivals can creep some people out a bit, but if you enjoy their fun and sparkling lights, the Musée des Arts Forains is a very special experience. This private collection of fun fair objects that date from 1850 to 1950 can be found right behind the Bercy Pavilions, a smidgen outside the border of Paris. This whimsical journey through the world of carnival — complete with can-can girls and feather plumes — is more than just a place to admire; you can play the games and go on the rides. Among them is a bicycle merry-go-round that makes everyone giggle like a kid again. To visit the museum, it's wise to sign up in advance for a tour, and the space can even be rented for private events.

RED HOUSE

Casual cocktails

1 Bis Rue de La Forge Royale (75011) / +33 1 43 67 06 43
facebook.com/pages/Red-House / Open daily

With its bull horns above the bar and its pinball machine, this bar seems more like a place to order a beer rather than a cocktail, but it surprisingly serves up some of the best mixes in Paris. It's hard to choose just one from the menu artfully scribbled on the mirror behind the bar, but I recommend you try the Wild West Side (tequila, chili, cucumber and lime), or, pardon my French, the F**king Legend (Mezcal, Chartreuse, falernum syrup, lime and mint). It's rare to find a joint where you can enjoy a fine cocktail in a laid-back setting, and that's precisely what I like about Red House.

parisian markets

Food, antiques and flowers take to the streets

Parisian markets are where you can take in some of the most vibrant displays of French culture. From local growers pitching their produce to quirky antiques dealers negotiating prices with customers, the fusion of characters and commerce is always entertaining.

When it comes to antiques, the **Porte de Vanves** was the first flea I ever went to in Paris, and to this day remains my favorite, all sentimentality aside. Here you'll find a vast array of treasures at fair prices, from furniture, to books, silver and vintage clothing. There is just enough to keep you busy without wasting a whole day. Another brocante I love is that in **Le Village Saint-Paul**. This is by no means the most extensive of the city's markets, but the ambiance the village lends to it is unlike any other. The shops and cafés lining the courtyards that make up the village are a great way to punctuate browsing the stands.

LE VILLAGE SAINT-PAUL
26 Rue Saint-Paul (75004), levillagesaintpaul.com
closed Wednesday, brocante open first weekend of
every month

MARCHÉ ALIGRE
Place d'Aligre (75012), +33 1 45 11 71 11
equipement.paris.fr/marche-couvert-beauvau-marche-d-
aligre-5480, closed Monday

MARCHÉ AUX FLEURS
Place Louis Lépine et Quai de la Corse (75004)
equipement.paris.fr/marche-aux-fleurs-et-aux-oiseaux-
cite-4506, open daily

MARCHÉ MONGE
Place Monge (75005), +33 1 48 85 93 30
equipement.paris.fr/marche-monge-5464
open Wednesday, Friday and Saturday

PORTE DE VANVES
Avenue Georges Lafenestre (75014), +33 6 86 89 99 96
placesdevanves.typepad.com, open Saturday and Sunday

For food, the **Marché Monge** at cobbled-stoned Rue Mouffetard and Place Monge is often regarded as Paris's quaintest, with shops and stands selling fresh produce, fish, pastries, and in autumn, wild game. For an even bigger selection, you can shop at the busy **Marché Aligre** beside some of the top local chefs. If you can't wait to get home and cook something up, you can buy a bite to eat right away from an array of what locals call "traiteurs".

There are specialty markets for nearly everything in Paris, and the **Marché aux Fleurs** and the bird market on the Île de la Cité might just be the most beguiling. Seven days a week, you can choose from a huge assortment of plants and flowers, and on Sunday, the bird vendors arrive with their most colorful feathered friends as well as exotic chickens and more.

the marais and île saint-louis

The first time I set foot in the Marais, it felt more like a movie set than a real place. Much in thanks to its medieval charms left largely untouched during Paris's Hausmannian renovations, it is perhaps the most historical and picturesque part of Paris. In the south, the Île Saint-Louis offers beautiful views of the Seine and is bridged by the Pont Louis-Philippe to the Right Bank and the Rue Vieille du Temple – the spine of the Marais. Just off it is the narrow and bustling Rue des Rosiers, filled with famous vintage shops and the self-proclaimed world's best falafel vendors. Work your way east and you'll end up at the Place des Vosges, the former brick palace surrounding a park now lined with galleries and cafés. While most of the action in the Marais used to take place in the 4th, the 3rd arrondissement, now poshly referred to as the Haute Marais, has boomed in recent years. Take your pick: any which way you go in the Marais, you will be delighted by its seemingly endless charms. After six years of calling this area home, I have never once grown tired of it.

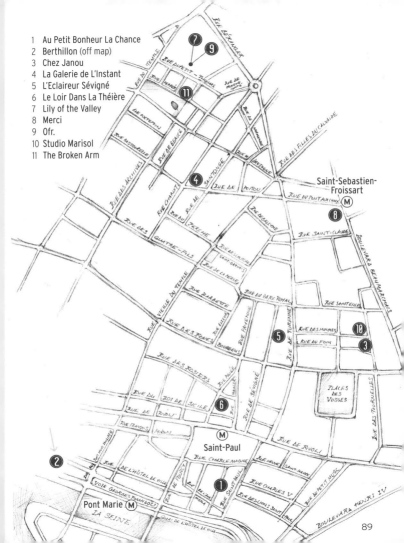

1 Au Petit Bonheur La Chance
2 Berthillon (off map)
3 Chez Janou
4 La Galerie de L'Instant
5 L'Eclaireur Sévigné
6 Le Loir Dans La Théière
7 Lily of the Valley
8 Merci
9 Ofr.
10 Studio Marisol
11 The Broken Arm

89

AU PETIT BONHEUR LA CHANCE

Chock-a-block with vintage

3 Rue Saint-Paul (75004) / +33 1 42 74 36 38 / No website
Closed Tuesday, Saturday and Sunday

The name of this little shop translates into English as "Haphazardly". While inside initially appears to hold a hodge-podge of all sorts, digging a bit further I find it hard to believe that each item is not a thoughtfully chosen remnant of someone's past. I mustn't neglect to point out the selection of small café bowls, which are quite a collector's item in Paris. You never know what you may find here, and that's the fun of it. From a pretty little embroidered hanky, to an old love letter, to vintage lunch boxes, to antique toys, there are treasures to be uncovered everywhere you look. Happy hunting!

BERTHILLON

The ice cream king of Paris

29-31 Rue Saint-Louis en l'Île (75004) / +33 1 43 54 31 61
berthillon.fr / Closed Monday and Tuesday

Berthillon serves the finest ice cream in Paris. This historic ice creamery has called the little Île Saint-Louis home since the 1960s. Ask nearly any Parisian, and they will tell you it's the best, and whatever the weather, sun or snow, they'll turn up to get their scoops here. All the ice cream is made below the shop, and their nougatine and caramels are homemade to this day. Get your cone to go, or sit down inside and order my choice, Belle-Hélène: a chocolate dipped pear teetering on a scoop of vanilla ice-cream and sprinkled with almond brittle.

CHEZ JANOU

Provençal bistrot

2 Rue Roger Verlomme (75003) / +33 1 42 72 28 41
chezjanou.com / Open daily

If there is any place that could steal my heart from Paris, it is Provence. While there is so much to love in the South of France, the food is definitely at the top of the list. Luckily for me though, in the city there is Chez Janou, just behind the Place de Vosges. Their Provençal cuisine brings back all my fondest summer memories of eating my way through the Luberon. If you're a fan of the south's anise-flavored aperitif, pastis, then this is the place in Paris to drink it. As in the south, the lamb here is a carnivore's delight, however it's served, and they're also known for their chocolate mousse, which is served à volonté, meaning (brilliantly) all you can eat!

LA GALERIE DE l'INSTANT

Famous faces framed

46 Rue de Poitou (75003) / +33 1 44 54 94 09
lagaleriedelinstant.com/home / Closed Monday

The ability to stop time in an instant with a camera, to capture a moment and keep it forever is, to me, close to magic. And La Galerie de l'Instant is filled with such wizardry in its collection of photographs, all of which are seemingly stolen moments from the private lives of some of the greatest personalities of all time. Icons like Steve McQueen, The Rolling Stones, Kate Moss, Brigitte Bardot, Marilyn Monroe, Serge Gainsbourg and Faye Dunaway are all recurring faces here in the archives from world renowned photographers and mystery snappers alike. It's always a pleasure to stop by to see old greats and uncover new favorites.

L'ECLAIREUR SÉVIGNÉ

Leaders in luxury

40 Rue de Sévigné (75003) / +33 1 48 87 10 22
leclaireur.com/en / Open daily

L'Eclaireur has gone through an evolution in its 30-year history.
Originally opened on the Champs-Élysées, its founders Armand and
Martine Hadida have been at the forefront of fashion in France, taking
chances on young designers, like Dries Van Noten and Martin Margiela
to name a few, well before they were household names. Today you'll
find the shop in the Marais, stocking a selection as bold as ever for both
men and women, of clothing and accessories. The garments and every
corner of the store are all works of art.

LE LOIR DANS LA THÉIÈRE

Country comfort food

3 Rue des Rosiers (75004) / +33 1 42 72 90 61 / No website
Open daily

Most people refer to Le Loir dans la Théiere as a tea room because the name is a reference to the dormouse that fell into the teapot in *Alice's Adventures in Wonderland*. Yet tea is not their specialty; it's the food — rustic and simple French country cooking, a lot like grandmère's. The sweets are to die for, but their savories are delicious, too. A daily choice of savory tarts (much like quiche), omelets with fresh mint, or the house club sandwich and fruit-filled tarte tatins will always make a great lunch. It's a wonderful place to cozy up and eat comfort food on a cold day in the Marais.

LILY OF THE VALLEY

Tea time in the Haute Marais

Rue Dupetit-Thouars (75003) / +33 1 57 40 82 80
fr-fr.facebook.com/lilyofthevalleyparis / Open daily

This dreamy little tea spot is a welcome addition to mix things up a bit after the recent influx of new coffee places in Paris. The narrow space is attractively utilized, with flowers and vines covering the ceilings and reflecting in the mirrored walls for a very fanciful effect. A floral bench divided with small tables is a lovely corner to cuddle up and admire the shelves of vintage mismatched dishes and their selection of teas. When the weather permits, tables in front get direct sunlight as well, making for another delightful place to sip on their organic French infusions.

MERCI

The home of Parisian bobo

111 Boulevard Beaumarchais (75003) / +33 1 42 77 00 33
merci-merci.com/en / Closed Sunday

Merci is the epicenter of bobo, or the "bohemian bourgeois" as we call them in France. Downstairs you can shop for kitchenware, and then dine on seasonal salads and homemade desserts while looking over their garden. Mid-level, you can outfit your closet with ultra hip French brands like Séssun, Carven and Isabel Marant, and grab a coffee or tea with a good read in the library. Upstairs, you can furnish any room of your house or find stylish office goods such as Japanese tape, because you know every bobo needs that sitting around their desk. Sometimes I feel so at home I find it hard to leave. But eventually I get what I need, say "merci!" and manage to go back to my real home.

OFR.

All things good on paper

20 rue Dupetit-Thouars (75003) / +33 1 42 45 72 88
ofrsystem.com / Open daily

Ofr. is our local ultra cool and multilingual book and paper shop in North Marais. It's also arguably the best in all of Paris with its wide range of guides, books and vast array of magazines on fashion, photography, art, design, architecture and more. You can tell by the selection right away that its founders are passionate about all of the above. Also up for grabs is a great assortment of candles, notebooks, scarves and other little gifts. Lastly, in the back you'll find their gallery dedicated to hosting rotating exhibitions by local artists and each time there's someone new, Ofr. hosts a friendly opening to which the public are welcome.

STUDIO MARISOL

The art of the French braid

33 Rue des Tournelles (75003) / +33 1 44 61 18 34
latresseparisienne.com / Open daily

Like most of my greatest Parisian discoveries, this one turned up on an aimless walk around the city. A selection of neon braided hair accessories in the window caught my eye. To my delight, I found the whole salon is dedicated to high fashion braiding. In addition to the hair clips, bands, crowns and more on sale inside, you can make an appointment to have your locks braided by studio founder Marisol herself, a woman who's passionate about braids. If I have a special event, it's my go-to salon to get my hair done and the elegant, unique updo can even last for a couple of days.

THE BROKEN ARM

Elevate the everyday

**12 Rue Perrée (75003) / +33 1 44 61 53 60 / the-broken-arm.com
Closed Sunday**

The Broken Arm is a hybrid space offering up all good things in life. In the café you'll find an organic seasonal menu updated every day with tasty fresh plates and home-baked goods. In their adjacent clothes shop catering to both men and women, brands such as Jacquemus, Cédric Charlier, Raf Simmons and a number of exclusive collaborations fill the racks. On the shelves are glossy magazines, photo books and even fragrances. The two-story space is bathed in light and has a minimalist but colorful design. I wish I could figure out why they call it The Broken Arm though, because certainly no one needs to break mine to go to this lovely place.

oyster bars

Paris's culinary pearls for seafood lovers

CLAMATO
80 Rue de Charonne (75011), +33 1 43 72 74 53
septime-charonne.fr, closed Monday and Tuesday

HUÎTRERIE RÉGIS
3 Rue de Montfaucon (75006), +33 1 44 41 10 07
huitrerieregis.com, closed Monday

LA CABANE À HUÎTRES
4 Rue Antoine Bourdelle (75015), +33 1 45 49 47 27
cabane-a-huitres.fr, closed Sunday through Tuesday

LE MARY CELESTE
1 Rue Commines (75003), +33 9 80 72 98 83
lemaryceleste.com, open daily

While Paris is landlocked, the shores of Normandy and Bretagne offering some of the finest fruits de mer are not far away. I tasted my first oyster in Paris late one night at an old fashioned brasserie and they have since become one of my favorite things to eat. I try to refrain in the months that don't contain a letter "R" but as soon as September rolls around, I'm back in search of them.

As of late I've been frequenting **Clamato**'s 20-foot bar, enjoying oysters on the half shell from Utah Beach or Maldon, and with their spicy homemade Tabasco sauce and shallot vinaigrette. The name comes from the famous clam juice, as you can imagine, but the only place you'll find that here is in their very good Bloody Mary.

At **Le Mary Celeste**, named after the maritime mystery of the abandoned ship and its vanished crew, the staff is still very much on board serving fresh seafood to go with their stunning cocktails, and dishes such as deviled eggs with pickled beets.

Huîtrerie Régis is a little culinary pearl on the Left Bank that takes pride in its oysters exclusively from Marennes d'Oléron, known for their refined nutty taste and blue-green gills.

If you want to get snug, try the local's pick, **La Cabane à Huîtres**. The communal tables and tight quarters (much like a ship's cabin) give it a family vibe, and your dinner is shucked before your eyes and served by the dozen.

————◆————

saint germain
and the
latin quarter

Saint Germain and The Latin Quarter are the center of the Left Bank. The 5th and 6th have gone down in history thanks to intellectuals of the Lost Generation and the Existentialists, but the district has also been home to many great artists, politicians and actors. Between the Seine River and the Luxembourg Gardens are squeezed some of the city's most famous cafés and shops. The Latin Quarter takes its name from the university crowds conversing in Latin here until the mid-century. Today, young families choose the 5th for its casual, calm surroundings. Around Odéon and Saint Germain des Près, the high-end price tag of the neighborhood is obvious from the luxury shops, exclusive galleries and the stylish lunchers that line the boulevards. Further south, past the beautiful Saint Sulpice church, Le Bon Marché department store and its Grand Epicerie at Sèvres Babylone will make you want to live the good life on the Left Bank. Yet the real charm of this area comes for free, via its exemplary Haussmannian architecture and fabulous parks.

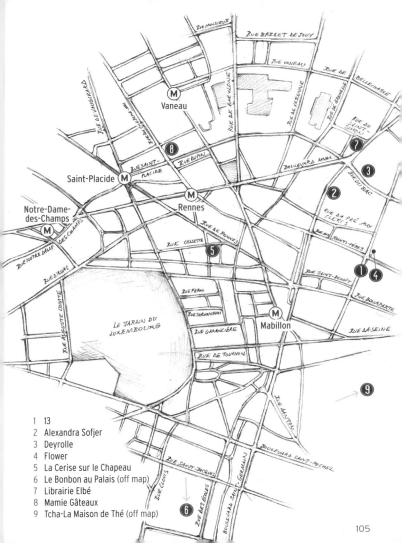

1 13
2 Alexandra Sofjer
3 Deyrolle
4 Flower
5 La Cerise sur le Chapeau
6 Le Bonbon au Palais (off map)
7 Librairie Elbé
8 Mamie Gâteaux
9 Tcha-La Maison de Thé (off map)

13

A baker's dozen

16 Rue des Saints-Pères (75007) / +33 1 73 77 27 89
facebook.com/treizeis13isthirteen / Closed Sunday and Monday

Twelve for the guests plus a well-deserved one for the accomplished cook makes a baker's dozen at 13 (Treize). This little eatery tucked away in a quiet courtyard is owned and run by a friendly "Frenchified" American who brings the best of her two worlds together in her home-style cooking. All the meat and veg are organic, the eggs are free range and the butter is fresh from the farm. Tasty savory pies like broccoli, mushroom and shrimp, and innovative salads are some of the delicious things you can enjoy on the barstools at their high-top tables. My eyes always go straight to the dessert counter, rotating a daily selection of some classics from home such as apple pie and carrot cake.

ALEXANDRA SOFJER

The art of umbrellas

218 Boulevard Saint-Germain (75007) / +33 1 42 22 17 02
alexandrasojfer.com / Closed Sunday

Alexandra Sofjer is a third-generation designer who decided to buy
one of Paris's oldest umbrella shops on Boulevard Saint-Germain in
2002 and has since grown it into the whimsical universe of fine objects
it is today. The store is filled with exceptionally designed umbrellas,
parasols, walking sticks and various leather goods such as gloves.
Alexandra uses the finest of materials including ostrich skin, ebony,
snakewood, organza, silk and crystals to assemble these elegant
objects that are part utilitarian and part works of art. After investing
in one of her pieces, rainy days don't seem half so gloomy anymore.

DEYROLLE

A menagerie of curiosity

46 Rue du Bac (75007) / +33 1 42 22 30 07 / deyrolle.com/en
Closed Sunday

Now, taxidermy might make a few people uneasy, but before I go any further, let me assure you that there was no cruelty involved in filling the Noah's Ark that is Deyrolle. The exotic creatures all died of natural causes, and were preserved in all their beauty by some of the world's leading taxidermists so we can get up close and personal with the curious collection. Polar bears, peacocks, butterflies and beetles are just some of the creatures big and small on display and for sale at this natural history museum of a shop. Stop in for a visit just to marvel, or for a pretty penny, take a giraffe or tiger home, if you fancy.

FLOWER

Exceptional florist

14 Rue des Saints-Pères (75006) / +33 1 44 50 00 20
flower.fr / Open daily

Nestled within a tiny shop on the Rue Saint-Pères is a grand florist blooming to the ceiling of its red tapestry-walled interior. A chipped Baroque mirror hangs on the wall, an old Singer sewing machine is used as a table, and antique medicine bottles and books are scattered throughout. The space feels like a room in a neglected Victorian mansion that's been overgrown by a secret garden; one filled with nearly forgotten varieties of roses, rare orchids and sought-after blooms from the foremost plantations. Their bouquets are grand, yet capture the simple beauty of nature, and as one of the finest florists in Paris, they are responsible for flowers you'll see throughout the city at many of its most stylish boutiques.

LA CERISE SUR LE CHAPEAU

Couture millinery

1 Rue Cassette (75006) / +33 1 45 49 90 53
lacerisesurlechapeau.com/en / Closed Sunday and Monday

From canotiers, to berets and bonnets, the French are people of many hats. In fact, I am one of them, as they're some of my favorite accessories. So I would know that the place to get headwear in Paris is La Cerise sur le Chapeau. What's so special? All the hats can be customized for you in store and, when the daily demand is not too high, completed right before your eyes. You can select from straw or wool options, and top them off with your choice of ribbons, feathers and other decorative touches. Just hand your selections to their hat makers and they'll whip everything together for you in no time.

LE BONBON AU PALAIS

Classic French confectionery

19 Rue Monge (75005) / +33 1 78 56 15 72 / bonbonsaupalais.fr
Closed Sunday and Monday

Georges, the owner of Le Bonbon au Palais, is a friendly Frenchman who is young at heart. In his charming shop, he's reimagined a 1950s classroom, but instead of studies we all get to eat candy. Not your typical Haribo gummies though, but rather the most delectable, authentically French sweets sourced from every region of the country. Old fashioned bonbons like almond and fruit calissons, fresh caramels, chocolates and guimauves (French marshmallows) are just some of the tasty things here that you can fill your bag with to savor while walking around the city.

LIBRAIRIE ELBÉ

Original vintage posters

**213 Boulevard Saint-Germain (75007) / +33 1 45 48 77 97
elbe-paris.fr / Closed Sunday**

Nearly 50 years on from the height of her career, and Brigitte Bardot is still turning heads. She's how I found Librairie Elbé in fact, as one day when walking up Boulevard Saint-Germain I spotted three giant posters in their window for the film *Une Parisienne* with B.B. featured front and center. Inside is an impressive collection of entirely original vintage posters, impeccably preserved I might add. Many of them are for classic French films, but there's also old promotional work for tourism, expositions and sports that today more closely resemble art than advertising.

MAMIE GÂTEAUX

Grandmother's kitchen

66 Rue du Cherche-Midi (75006) / +33 1 42 22 32 15
mamie-gateaux.com/index.htm / Closed Sunday and Monday

Grand-mère is in the kitchen and I like what she's cooking.
At Mamie Gâteaux you can have more than grandma's cakes, but
also her appetizing brunch, salads, tarts, teas, cookies, coffee and
more. Everyone feels looked after here in this comfy and cute little café
in the 6th arrondissement. The menu is hearty and simple; like you
would expect from grand-mère. The space is decorated with antique
cookie and tea jars, and the retro school-house chairs and desks make
you feel like a kid again. This is a great place to cozy up on your own
for some comfort food and TLC, and is also family friendly for those
with kids. On the way out, you can even shop for kitchenware in the
boutique. Allez! To granny's kitchen we go.

TCHA-LA MAISON DE THÉ

A tranquil tea room

**6 Rue du Pont de Lodi (75006) / +33 1 43 29 61 31 / No website
Closed Monday**

Tcha-La Maison de Thé is an authentic Asian tea room just a stone's throw from Place Saint Michel. For those seeking calm in the bustle of the city, the salon is ultra quiet with peaceful silence broken only by soft harp music or the gentle whispers of the managing family as they serve you. An extensive list of white, green and black leaves, with delights such as white lychee or green peony, come served in dinky little pots for brewing only one cup at a time. The large thermos accompanying your tea service is to replenish your pot for a perfectly steeped cup each time, but as the staff will kindly remind you, don't let it brew for more than three minutes! At lunchtime, tempting savory dishes are on the menu, and in the late afternoon, sweet treats like ginger or soy biscuits are served to accompany your cuppa.

les grands pâtissiers

The sweetest treats on Paris's pastry scene

COLOROVA
47 Rue de l'Abbé Grégoire (75006), +33 1 45 44 67 56
facebook.com/Colorova75006, closed Monday

L'ÉCLAIR DE GÉNIE
14 Rue Pavée (75004), +33 1 42 77 85 11
leclairdegenie.com, open daily

ODETTE
77 Rue Galande (75005), +33 1 43 26 13 06
odette-paris.com, open daily

SÉBASTIEN GAUDARD
22 Rue des Martyrs (75009), +33 1 71 18 24 70
sebastiengaudard.fr, closed Monday

It's hard not to eat your heart out in Paris. With so many tempting delicacies at every turn, it's a miracle the population stays so slim. Trust me though, the locals do indulge. The secret is in the amount of walking they do. So if you do want to eat up, prepare to do likewise.

I stumbled upon **Sébastien Gaudard** by chance walking down the Rue des Martyrs one day. The most impeccable cake in the form of Marie Antoinette in the window lured me in. Tasting Gaudard's versions of France's greatest desserts, from the éclair to the Paris Brest, is a great way to relish a sugar rush.

Speaking of éclairs, at **L'Éclair de Génie**, Christophe Adam has given them a 21st-century twist. Colorful rows of new flavors like passion fruit milk chocolate, creamy fig, lemon yuzu and more look and taste heavenly. I love to grab a few with a friend and eat them nearby on the banks of the Seine. Also bringing a bit of modernity to French pastries, the so called "neo bakery", **Colorova** on the Left Bank has some of the most stylish contemporary sweet creations. Chocolate cake layered with ganache and passion fruit cream, or speculoos and peanut mousse tarts are enough to make your mouth water.

If you like your desserts bite-sized, visit **Odette** and pop some pâte à choux in your mouth. The owners rely on their grandmother's recipe and from what I have tasted, they are making her proud.

———◆———

eiffel and trocadéro

The key attraction of this neighborhood is perhaps the main draw in all of France: the Eiffel Tower. I've spent a good amount of time sitting on the Champs de Mars splayed out in front of it and, call me cheesy, but I never tire of it. The view from Place du Trocadéro, just across the river on the Right Bank, is one of the most iconic in the world. The surrounding neighborhoods, and that of Eiffel on the same side of the river, are indeed lovely corners of the city. These areas have always been the home of the aristocracy and French bourgeois, and while sometimes uppity, it's what makes them chic and calm once you're off the main roads. Although there are some good venues here, the district isn't as diverse or rich in terms of shopping and dining as other parts of the city. So the main pull here is the Eiffel Tower after all, and that's a wonderful thing because should you find yourself nearby, you can take it in at your leisure without fear of missing out on other sights.

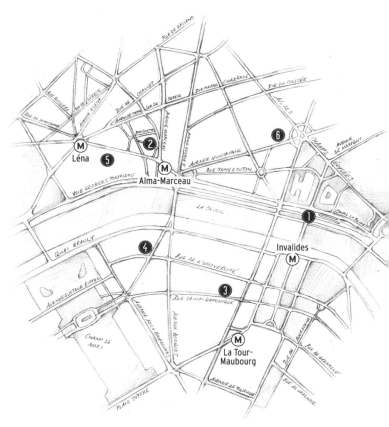

1 Faust
2 Fondation Pierre Bergé – Yves Saint Laurent
3 Le Moulin de la Vierge
4 Les Deux Abeilles
5 Librairie du Palais de Tokyo
6 Montaigne Market

FAUST

Cool kids club

Invalides (75007) / +33 1 44 18 60 60 / faustparis.fr/en / Open daily

Faust is a welcome new addition to the Eiffel area, if you ask me.
The neighborhood can be a bit sleepy as the young crowd tends to hug
the Right Bank for a good night out. Thanks to the artistic direction of
Charaf Tanger and James Whelan, who are known to throw a good party,
Faust is now a bright spot on the Left Bank. Sip away an afternoon on
the terrace underneath the magnificent Pont Alexandre III with a view
of the Eiffel Tower and stay for dinner at the brasserie to enjoy Michelin-
starred chef Christophe Langrée's cuisine. And the party I mentioned?
It all happens in "The Tunnel" where you can find up-and-coming
international DJs entertaining the cool crowd.

FONDATION PIERRE BERGÉ – YVES SAINT LAURENT

Ode to YSL

5 Avenue Marceau (75116) / +33 1 44 31 64 00 / fondation-pb-ysl.net
Closed Monday

I truly believe one of the greatest love stories of all time is that of Yves Saint Laurent and Pierre Bergé. Their yin and yang in love, life and fashion emanates from the medley of YSL mementos and work here. Bergé said "If Chanel gave women their freedom, it was Saint Laurent who empowered them", and in the 81 haute couture collections presented across 1,283 production boards here, you can see how. You can also view selected photographs and pieces from his couture and ready-to-wear collections. This small museum is a must visit for any fashion lover.

LE MOULIN DE LA VIERGE

A beautiful bakery

64 Rue Saint-Dominique (75007) / +33 1 40 52 55 55
lavierge.com / Closed Wednesday

There are a lot of wonderful bakeries in Paris, but few are officially classified as historical monuments like Le Moulin de la Vierge. I was first introduced to it when I was going to school in this neighborhood and my French class took a field trip here. Bribing us with croissants, brioche and baguettes was a good way to force us to speak French. I said "s'il vous plaît" right away to this carbohydrate heaven and still find it to be the most exquisite bakery in all of Paris, with its old fashioned façade, elegant lamps, wood and marble display cases, and ceiling mural all from the Belle Epoque. It's truly a landmark in the neighborhood and a treasured stop in the daily lives of the locals.

LES DEUX ABEILLES

Where locals lunch

189 Rue de l'Université (75007) / +33 1 45 55 64 04 / No website
Closed Sunday

The mother and daughter duo running this lunch and tea gem have
nicknamed themselves "the two little bees". It's fitting because when lunch
hour rolls around, they are buzzing about, serving a full house eager to
drink and dine. Even at just a stone's throw from the Eiffel Tower, the place
goes largely undiscovered by tourists. Instead you'll find the quartier's
bourgeois locals inside, a good sign that the food is excellent. The meals
are light and fresh: sliced chicken on a bed of greens lightly dressed
and topped with pine nuts or a tarte tatin à la tomate, for example.
The limited wine list makes the choice easy, as it's meticulously paired with
the menu. You can also stop in for just tea and desserts later in the day.

LIBRAIRIE DU PALAIS DE TOKYO

Contemporary bookshop

13 Avenue du Président Wilson (75116) / +33 1 49 52 02 04
palaisdetokyo.com / Closed Tuesday

Once I've visited a big Paris museum, I sort of have a "been there, done that" attitude for a few years before returning. The Palais de Tokyo, however, has a few perks that keep me coming back often. In addition to its café and terrace with a lovely view of the Seine and Eiffel Tower, I love popping into the book and gift shop, especially after the shows here during Fashion Week. The unique and cheerful bookstore is a glossy library of contemporary art, fashion, music and architecture. It's open until midnight, making it a perfect late night cultural stop after a nice dinner at Trocadéro and taking in the twinkling lights of the Eiffel Tower view there.

MONTAIGNE MARKET

Luxury designer fashion

57 Avenue Montaigne (75008) / +33 1 42 56 58 58
montaignemarket.com / Closed Sunday

When I make it big, Avenue Montaigne will be my first stop to spend my hard won cash. Calmer and classier than the neighboring Champs-Élysées, it's home to some of the most exclusive shopping in the world, being lined with luxury flagships. The best of all those brands seem to come together at Montaigne Market, with a reliably on-trend collection of the season's optimum pieces from the likes of Givenchy, Alaïa and Simone Rocha. With ensembles up to the standards of any voguette or fashion editor, it's the place to find the It bag or must-have shoes, and learn how to dress head-to-toe to be the next street style star.

en plein air

Great walks and beautiful parks for a breath of fresh air

BOIS DE BOULOGNE
Between Allée du Bord de l'Eau and
Allée de Fortifications, +33 1 53 92 82 82, open daily

BUTTES-CHAUMONT
1 Rue Botzaris (75019), +33 1 48 03 83 10
open daily

LA PROMENADE PLANTÉE
Quinze-Vingts (75012), promenade-plantee.org
open daily

LE JARDIN DES PLANTES
57 Rue Cuvier (75005), +33 1 40 79 56 01
jardindesplantes.net, open daily

QUAI RIVE DROITE
Pont Marie (75004), open Sunday

BUTTES-CHAUMONT

When the weather permits, Paris lends itself to a seemingly endless amount of outdoor activities. It is extremely easy to get around on foot, and the city is filled with some of the world's prettiest and well kept parks.

One of the largest is the **Bois de Boulogne**, bordering the chic upper class neighborhood of the 16th in the west. It's a lush refuge for those who come from all over Paris to enjoy it, myself included. Strolling its forest paths you can enjoy streams, small lakes (where you may hire boats to row away an afternoon), cafés, greenhouses and even a racetrack. On the other side of town, **Le Jardin des Plantes** in the 5th arrondissement pays true homage to nature. Covering 28 hectares, it's home to museums that cover entomology, paleontology and mineralogy. But my favorite thing to visit here is the tiny zoo where you can wonder at the animal descendants of Versailles' very own royal menagerie. In the north east of Paris, the park to see is the **Buttes-Chaumont**. In the center atop a rock, sits an idyllic lookout point where you can enjoy a 360-degree view of Paris. I've spent so many summer days here taking in all the season has to offer, sunning on the grass-covered hills, sipping rosé with friends and finishing the day with a snack or more drinks at the jolly Rosa Bonheur.

LA PROMENADE PLANTÉE

When it comes to walking, one of the greatest things about central Paris on the weekend is that pedestrians rule. Nowhere is this more evident than on the **Quai Rive Droite** each Sunday, as the highway is closed to cars and open for only cyclists, joggers, rollerbladers and everyone in between, who are allowed free run of the lanes lining the Seine. In summer, food vendors add some extra flavor to the banks with gelato and other carts. Also good for a stroll is **La Promenade Plantée**, sometimes equated to New York City's Highline as it also utilizes an obsolete railway track as a lush path, traversing Paris's 12th arrondissement. I stumbled upon it by chance at its origin of some inconspicuous stairs not far from Bastille. Curious, I followed it all the way to the end, and the leafy footpath has since become one of my most-loved walks in Paris.